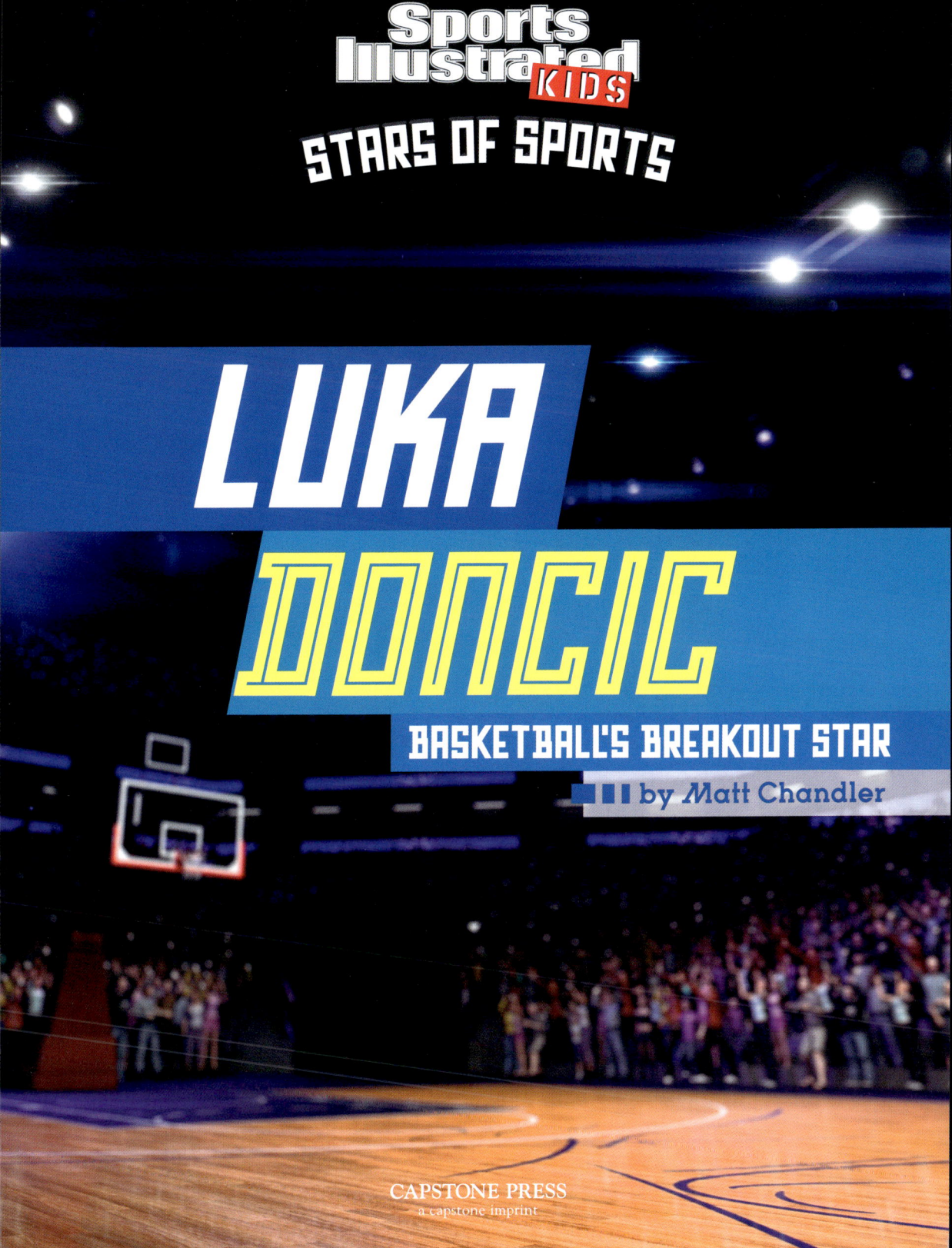

Stars of Sports is published by
Capstone Press, an imprint of Capstone
1710 Roe Crest Drive, North Mankato, Minnesota 56003
www.capstonepub.com

Copyright © 2022 by Capstone. All rights reserved. No part of this publication may be reproduced in whole or in part, or stored in a retrieval system, or transmitted in any form or by any means, electronic, mechanical, photocopying, recording, or otherwise, without written permission of the publisher.

SPORTS ILLUSTRATED KIDS is a trademark of ABG-SI LLC. Used with permission.

Library of Congress Cataloging-in-Publication Data
Names: Chandler, Matt, author.
Title: Luka Dončić : basketball's breakout star / Matt Chandler.
Description: North Mankato, Minnesota : Capstone Press, an imprint of Capstone, [2022] | Series: Sports illustrated kids stars of sports | Includes bibliographical references and index. | Audience: Ages 8-11 | Audience: Grades 4-6 |
Summary: "Slovenian basketball star Luka Doncic's talent was obvious from an early age. He went from playing in the EuroLeague to the NBA all by the young age of 19. Readers will learn about his struggles and successes on his way to becoming a star player and the NBA Rookie of the Year!"— Provided by publisher.
Identifiers: LCCN 2021008468 (print) | LCCN 2021008469 (ebook) | ISBN 9781663907271 (Hardcover) | ISBN 9781663907240 (PDF) | ISBN 9781663907264 (Kindle Edition)
Subjects: LCSH: Dončić, Luka—Juvenile literature. | Basketball players—Slovenia—Juvenile literature.
Classification: LCC GV884.D645 C53 2022 (print) | LCC GV884.D645 (ebook) | DDC 796.223092 [B]—dc23
LC record available at https://lccn.loc.gov/2021008468
LC ebook record available at https://lccn.loc.gov/2021008469

Editorial Credits
Editor: Mandy Robbins; Designer: Dina Her; Media Researcher: Morgan Walters; Production Specialist: Tori Abraham

Image Credits
Associated Press: Albert Pena/CSM via ZUMA Wire, 17, Brian Rothmuller/Icon Sportswire, 5, Kevin C. Cox/Pool Photo, 24, 27, Kevin Hagen, 16, Kim Klement, 23, Matt York, 19, Ray Carlin, 21, Ron Jenkins, 28; Getty Images: Francesco Richieri, 8, Rodolfo Molina, 13; Newscom: Brian Rothmuller/Icon Sportswire, Cover, Juan Carlos García Mate / Pacific Press, 11, Shot for Press/Action Plus, 14, Vid Ponikvar/Sportida, 6; Shutterstock: Chansom Pantip, 20, Oleksii Sidorov, 1, xbrchx, 7

All internet sites appearing in back matter were available and accurate when this book was sent to press.

TABLE OF CONTENTS

PLAYOFF POWER 4

CHAPTER ONE
CHILDHOOD SUPERSTAR 6

CHAPTER TWO
REAL MADRID 10

CHAPTER THREE
NBA DREAMS 16

CHAPTER FOUR
FROM ROOKIE TO POWERHOUSE 20

CHAPTER FIVE
A BRIGHT FUTURE 26

TIMELINE 29
GLOSSARY 30
READ MORE 31
INTERNET SITES 31
INDEX 32

Words in **BOLD** are in the glossary.

PLAYOFF POWER

The Los Angeles Clippers jumped out to a quick 10–0 lead over the Dallas Mavericks. It was Game One of the 2019–20 National Basketball Association (NBA) Playoffs. The Mavericks needed someone to step up.

Luka Doncic brought the ball down court. Suddenly, he broke for the basket. Doncic weaved between defenders and scored a layup. It was the beginning of a huge night for Doncic. He was playing in his first NBA playoff game. Doncic made 13 shots from the floor. He added 14 free throws and finished the game with 42 points! Unfortunately, it wasn't enough to stop the Clippers. The Mavericks lost 118–110. But Doncic did set an NBA record for most points scored in a player's first NBA playoff game.

>>> Doncic puts up a shot against the Los Angeles Clippers in a February 25, 2019 game.

CHAPTER ONE
CHILDHOOD SUPERSTAR

Luka Doncic was born on February 28, 1999, in Slovenia. He was the only child of Mirjam and Sasa Doncic. Doncic's parents divorced when he was young. Sasa was also a basketball player. He taught his son the game at an early age. Doncic was holding a basketball before he could even walk. He didn't join his first team until he was seven years old. But he watched and learned the game from his dad.

>>> Doncic and his father

In 2007, Sasa Doncic signed to play on the Union Olimpija team. Luka was eight years old. He joined a lower level Union Olimpija team with his dad. It was with this team that Luka's **elite** talent as a basketball player first developed. Union Olympija's coach started Doncic practicing with the eight-year-old team. His training had officially begun.

Life in Slovenia

Today, Doncic plays basketball in Dallas, Texas, 5,500 miles (8,851 kilometers) from where he was raised in Slovenia. He grew up speaking Slovenian. He enjoyed foods of his native land such as potato moussaka. But much of his life in Slovenia was just like a typical American childhood. His favorite thing to do was shoot hoops every day. He loved his dog, and he dreamed of being a basketball player when he grew up.

>>> Doncic takes a shot for Real Madrid during the Adidas Next Generation tournament in 2015.

Doncic practiced once with the eight-year-old team. The coaches quickly realized he was too good. They moved him up to play with the older players. After a single practice with players three years older than him, Doncic was still the best player on the court. Once again, the coaches advanced him.

"I was always training and playing with older kids who had much more experience than me," Doncic once said. "Many of them were bigger and faster than me too, so I had to beat them with my brain."

By the time he was 12 years old, Doncic was already 6 feet 2 inches (188 centimeters) tall. His height and ball-handling skills helped him be the best player on his team. Doncic was 13 years old when he signed a five-year contract to play for professional team Real Madrid!

FACT

Doncic worked as a ball boy for his dad's Slovenian League basketball team. He watched and learned from some of the best basketball players in his country.

CHAPTER TWO
REAL MADRID

Doncic left his home in Slovenia and moved to Spain to play with the Real Madrid's youth academy. It was tough to be so far away from home without his family. His mom tried to talk Doncic out of playing in Spain.

"In the beginning, honestly, I said, Luka, you're really good. You have time," she said. "You can go later."

Doncic didn't want to wait. Once he arrived in Spain, he realized how tough the change was going to be.

"All my friends, school, family—everything was in Slovenia," he said.

FACT

Doncic speaks four languages—Serbian, Slovenian, Spanish, and English.

>>> Doncic gets physical playing for Real Madrid in a 2017 game.

Doncic did his best to focus on basketball. He trained and played in Real Madrid's youth academy. By 2015, he was ready to play in his first professional game!

SUPERSTAR IN SPAIN

Doncic played his first professional game on April 30, 2015. Real Madrid was taking on its Spanish League rival, Unicaja Malaga. With Real Madrid leading by 18 points, the coach put young Doncic in the game. With about a minute left, Doncic raced down the court and took a pass in the corner. The teen launched a smooth three pointer. The shot was a perfect swish! Doncic had scored his first professional basket.

Doncic continued to improve. One of his biggest moments came when Real Madrid was taking on FC Barcelona in 2017. With one second left in the third period, 18-year-old Doncic took the inbound pass. He launched the ball the entire length of the court. He nailed the shot to end the quarter!

>>> Doncic in action during a 2016 Real Madrid game against FC Barcelona.

The Business of Basketball

Doncic signed his first professional contract when he was 13 years old! That gave him years to develop his skills before joining the NBA. In America, professional leagues are not allowed to sign children. To play in the NBA, a player must be 19 years old. The NBA also runs two other professional leagues. They are called the G League and the 2K League. In both leagues, players must be at least 18 years old. European leagues don't have these rules.

>>> Doncic receives the 2018 Most Valuable Player award.

FACT

Doncic was named Most Valuable Player of the 2018 EuroLeague Final Four.

BREAKOUT SEASON

Doncic's breakout season came in 2018. In 33 games in EuroLeague competition, he averaged 16 points per game. He added nearly five **rebounds** and four **assists** per game.

It was in the EuroLeague playoffs where Doncic played his best basketball. He needed to play big if they were going to win the championship. Real Madrid easily beat CSKA Moscow in the semifinals.

They squared off against a team called Fenerbahce Dogus Istanbul for the EuroLeague Championship. Fenerbahce's defenders were all over Doncic for most of the game. They were determined not to let him beat them with his deadly three-point shot. Instead, he drew lots of fouls. Doncic hit eight of 10 free throws and finished the game with 15 points. Real Madrid won the EuroLeague Championship with an 85–80 victory!

CHAPTER THREE
NBA DREAMS

Doncic was one of the most talked-about players leading up to the 2018 **NBA Draft**. Some experts thought he was a lock to be the first pick. As draft day got closer, many thought some teams would select an American ahead of Doncic. In the end, he was chosen with the third pick by the Atlanta Hawks.

>>> Doncic poses with NBA Commissioner Adam Silver after being picked by the Atlanta Hawks during the 2018 NBA Draft.

>>> Doncic poses in his Dallas Mavericks jersey.

The Hawks didn't plan to keep Doncic, however. Before he even touched an NBA basketball, Doncic was traded to the Dallas Mavericks. The Mavs gave up two first round draft picks to land the superstar.

On July 10, 2018, Doncic signed with the Mavericks. His **rookie** contract was worth up to $32.6 million!

ROOKIE SENSATION

Some scouts worried Doncic would have a tough time adjusting to the NBA game. Would he have a hard time being so far from home? Would he struggle in a different culture with a new language? Could he compete against the best players in the world? Doncic proved right away he belonged in the NBA. He played his first NBA game on October 17, 2018. The Mavericks played the Phoenix Suns. Just two minutes into the game, Doncic took a pass from teammate J.J. Barea. The rookie softly laid in the shot for the first points of his NBA career! He went on to finish his first game with 10 points, eight rebounds and four assists.

Doncic started 72 games in his rookie season with the Mavericks. He finished the season averaging more than 21 points per game and was named the NBA Rookie of the Year.

>>> Doncic takes a shot against Tyson Chandler of the Phoenix Suns.

CHAPTER FOUR
FROM ROOKIE TO POWERHOUSE

Doncic's second season was a challenging one for the NBA and its players. **COVID-19** was spreading in the United States. Players were worried the season would be cancelled. Despite the stress, Doncic played great offensive basketball. He averaged more than 32 points per game in November and 26.1 points per game in December. The Mavs built a 19–10 record.

>>> Many businesses were closed due to the COVID-19 pandemic.

The NBA finally paused the season on March 11, 2020. They wanted to keep the players safe from COVID-19. It would be four months before they returned to finish the season. Doncic said it was a tough time for him.

"I always wanted to play," Doncic said when the season started again. "I missed basketball a lot, so I just wanted to play."

LIFE IN THE BUBBLE

To keep the players safe, the NBA moved all of the playoff teams to Orlando, Florida, to finish the season. The all lived and played together. The hope was that a **quarantine** would keep the players safe. It also made it difficult, because they could not see family and friends. For Doncic, it was something he was used to.

"For me, it's like some European championship," Doncic said at the time. "Every team is in the same hotel . . . I'm used to that . . . so it's not bad."

The Mavs struggled in the bubble, finishing the season by losing five of their last seven games. But Doncic continued to dominate. He averaged 30 points per game. He put up three **triple doubles** in his seven regular-season games in the bubble.

FACT

Doncic became the youngest player in NBA history to deliver a 30-point, 20-rebound triple double. He was 21 years, 158 days old.

>>> Doncic shoots a 3-pointer against Sacramento Kings guard Cory Joseph.

>>> Doncic takes a 3-point shot during Game 4 of the first round of the 2020 NBA Playoffs.

PLAYOFFS!

Doncic's strong second season helped lead the Mavericks to the NBA Playoffs. It was his first time playing in an NBA playoff game. But the young superstar had plenty of playoff experience playing in Europe. He led the Mavericks on offense. Doncic averaged 31 points and nearly 10 rebounds per game in the series.

It was his **buzzer beater** in Game Four that was the series highlight. With 3.7 seconds left in the game, the Mavs trailed the Clippers 133–132. Doncic was their last hope. He took the inbounds pass from Dorian Finney-Smith. At the last second he launched a long three-point shot. The shot went in. The Mavs won the game!

CHAPTER FIVE
A BRIGHT FUTURE

Doncic is already a superstar scorer in the NBA. But his defensive skills are not as strong. Experts say he is often slow to react to the player he is guarding.

His defensive weakness hurt the Mavericks in the 2019-20 playoffs. Doncic was matched up against Los Angeles Clippers superstar Kawhi Leonard. Doncic struggled to guard Leonard, who led his team in scoring in every game of the series. The Clippers beat the Mavericks 4–2 to win the series.

Doncic knows he has to improve his defense if he wants to lead the Mavs to an NBA Championship. "I think you can improve everything by the day," Doncic said. "You can't be satisfied by what you have."

>>> Doncic defends Kawhi Leonard of the Los Angeles Clippers.

JUST GETTING STARTED

Doncic is still a young player. He is still learning the game. He has proven that he is an elite player on offense. But some basketball experts point to his struggles on defense as proof that he still has a long way to go to be a superstar. Doncic knows he has work to do if he wants to be the best player in the NBA.

"Every year I want to be better, that's the goal," he said. "For me, like I always say, I want to win the championship."

>>> Doncic celebrates during a game against the Minnesota Timberwolves.